Ambiguous Spaces

NaJa & deOstos

Nannette Jackowski and Ricardo de Ostos

Princeton Architectural Press / New York

Published by
Princeton Architectural Press
37 East Seventh Street
New York, New York 10003

For a free catalog of books, call 1.800.722.6657.
Visit our website at www.papress.com.

Editor: Linda Lee
Designer: NaJa & deOstos

Special thanks to: Nettie Aljian, Sara Bader, Dorothy
Ball, Nicola Bednarek, Janet Behning, Becca Casbon,
Carina Cha, Penny (Yuen Pik) Chu, Russell Fernandez,
Pete Fitzpatrick, Wendy Fuller, Jan Haux, Clare
Jacobson, Aileen Kwun, Nancy Eklund Later, Aaron
Lim, Laurie Manfra, Katharine Myers, Lauren Nelson
Packard, Jennifer Thompson, Arnoud Verhaeghe, Paul
Wagner, Joseph Weston, and Deb Wood of Princeton
Architectural Press —Kevin C. Lippert, publisher

Library of Congress Cataloging-in-Publication Data

Jackowski, Nannette.
   Ambiguous spaces : NaJa & deOstos / Nannette
Jackowski and Ricardo de Ostos.
      p. cm. — (Pamphlet architecture ; 29)
   Includes bibliographical references.
   ISBN 978-1-56898-795-8 (pbk. : alk. paper)
   1. NaJa & deOstos (Firm) 2. Architecture, Modern—
21st century. 3. Symbolism in architecture. I. Ostos,
Ricardo de. II. Title.
   NA997.N24J333 2008
   720.92'2—dc22
                              2008020574

Contents

Foreword

Many readers of this book will wonder how exactly it relates to architecture. While its authors, Nannette Jackowski and Ricardo de Ostos (NaJa & deOstos), speak like designers—invoking various processes of shaping spaces and basing them on programmatic narratives—we quickly discover that they do not pursue any anticipated or logical idea of human habitation. Their projects do not provide the results we expect from architecture—shelter for people, aesthetic enjoyment, an armature for dialogue between people in a particular community—nor do they seek, or claim, to enhance an existing mode of living, foster progress, or in any other way improve the human condition. Rather, their projects are indifferent to the established approach to architecture and its implicit demands for accessibility. NaJa & deOstos creates what amounts to an alternative world in which we, with our assumptions and expectations, are strangers.

Over the past few decades, architecture as an idea and practice has increasingly limited its definition of itself. In the foreseeable future, the instrumentality of architecture in effecting actual change—that is, change that challenges the dominance of commercial institutions, their aims, and values—will diminish. While the present day seems to be a time of unparalleled innovation and freedom of choice, the reality is that architectural styles and forms are often the seductive packaging and repackaging of the same proven, marketable concepts. The speed with which "radical" designs by celebrity architects achieve acceptance and popularity demonstrates that formal innovation has itself become an important commodity. However, beneath the cloak of radicalism, the conventions of existing building typologies and programs, with all their comforting familiarity, still rule—and sell. What is needed desperately today are approaches to architecture that can free its potential to transform our ways of thinking, and acting.

The starting point for NaJa & deOstos is not political —the announcement of a new set of goals—or formal —the insistence on a new set of forms—but programmatic—a reframing of architecture's human content expressed in entirely new ways. The generators of their projects are site-specific narratives that weave together a bevy of oppositions: fact/fiction, objective/subjective, technological/natural, rational/magical. These written structures integrate the contradictions with equanimity, creating what their authors understatedly call ambiguity, an existential field of unpredictable potentials. The writings of Franz Kafka and Gabriel García Márquez are used as models and remind us that reality is not only complex but paradoxical, especially at the fracture line between what we think we know and what we actually know. The narratives set in motion a series of developments that seem both inexplicable and inevitable; by the time architecture arrives in the project, it is no longer the product of an established way of solving things—even less of the architect's purpose—but of a collision between intention and accident, desire and fear, the wondrous and the terrible.

NaJa & deOstos has invented a consequential architecture, a deeply ethical one. It is an architecture we have not seen before and not an easy one to understand or co-opt for marketing purposes. In its genuine uniqueness, it offers us new ways of thinking and working, and, thus, a truly hopeful, if difficult, way forward.

Lebbeus Woods
New York City, April 2008

Literary vs. Literal Architecture: NaJa & deOstos, or the Poetry of Infrastructure

By believing passionately in something that still does not exist, we create it. The nonexistent is whatever we have not sufficiently desired.

—Franz Kafka

Desire and imagination permeate the poetic imagery of *The Pregnant Island* and *Nuclear Breeding* by Nannette Jackowski and Ricardo de Ostos (NaJa & deOstos). These are projects infused with literary, no less than architectural, ambition and hint at an important generational return to architecture pursued, and understood, as a form of language. Avoiding all the obvious retro-semiotic and post-post-structural clichés, these are investigations that reveal architecture as an unexpectedly contemporary form of narrative and storytelling—something otherwise nearly impossible to imagine in our era of mass media, instantaneous information, and rampant develop-ment and urbanization. NaJa & deOstos pursues an architecture that is designed—and, more importantly, designed to speculate—on the unexpected strangeness, the otherworldliness of how human beings have already transformed their world through infrastructural modernization. It is important architectural work that takes as its site the most prosaic and ordinary feature of our planet: large-scale infrastructures. Bringing a poetic vision to the complexities of infrastructures and the sometimes-paradoxical consequences of their logics is one of the most surprising and beautiful aspects of their work.

NaJa & deOstos's architectural attention is focused on the unexpectedly alien (non-)places created by large-scale infrastructures of all kinds: artificial systems, engineered sites, and post-industrial/military terrains that (like Foucault's heterotopias) operate somewhere between (or outside) the conventional spaces of our everyday world. In the case of *The Pregnant Island* and *Nuclear Breeding*, these spaces are neither conventional landscapes nor building sites. This is one of the subtle differences that distinguish those projects from, for example,

the brilliant infrastructural installations and writings of an artist like Robert Smithson, whose work with airports, disused industrial landscapes, and mining sites suggests an obvious and important generational precursor to the work here. The (non-)places engaged by NaJa & deOstos in the two projects are considerably stranger, and more bizarre: the result of understanding the world through a kind of magical realism the architects themselves associate with the literary work of Gabriel García Márquez, Philip K. Dick, and others.

The Pregnant Island and *Nuclear Breeding* are evocative in their imagery as *literary* spaces. They also, of course, operate as *literal* proposals in the more conventional architectural sense, as projects that consist of a series of stunning drawings and models that depict—like all architectural representations—some space other than the graphics or texts themselves. As such, we are confronted with a rare example within architecture of the kinds of imaginary spaces perhaps best known now through recent generations of writers who take on space, experience, and perception; Paul Auster, Georges Perec, and the Oulipo group all come to mind as systematic literary explorers of the boundaries of the space of everyday life.

The two projects were developed by their architects/authors around two incredibly odd, nearly surreal, infrastructural sites. One is a vast expanse of more recent times and the other, an installation created at the height of the cold war, from more than fifty years ago. The former is the insanely huge Tucuruí Reservoir system completed in Pará, Brazil—the site of NaJa & deOstos's *The Pregnant Island*. When completed in the 1980s, Tucuruí, carved out of the heart of a tropical rain forest in ways that utterly overwhelmed local cultures and natural conditions, was the world's largest man-made lake. *Nuclear Breeding*, in contrast, is located half a world away in southeast England at the disused military site Orford Ness, originally created for a series of experimental tests leading to the British development of atomic weapons in the 1950s.

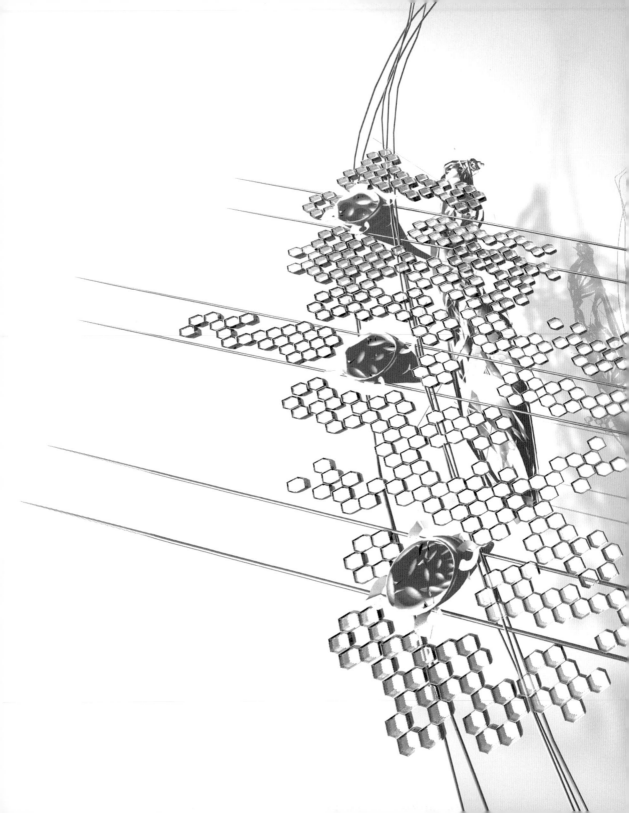

Let's just admit this at the beginning: a more unusual pair of sites selected to criticize the culture of contemporary architecture and building programs can hardly be imagined today. NaJa & deOstos brings to their exploration of these two super-weird locations a series of atmospheric drawings, models, diagrams, and written texts, all of which blend together into a special kind of architectural narrative or storytelling that allows the reader to see the outer limits of our existing planet in new, sometimes shocking, and wholly unexpected ways. The projects accomplish something even more important by pointing to a unique capacity for architecture to uncover as well as tell stories. This surprising architectural enterprise is made possible by the entirely "open brief" and self-invented purpose of these projects, which—in pursuit of their own occasionally surreal goal—go to great extremes to avoid the kind of market-satisfying function that defines so much of contemporary architectural design and thinking.

We live in a time in which contemporary architectural culture has nearly surrendered itself to the pervasive circumstances of global economies and the imperatives of their accelerating markets, technologies, and development. Architectural culture is, undoubtedly, growing more and more global, generic, and market driven. Questions of architectural vision and its necessity are, perhaps for the first time in a generation, beginning to swing back into the larger architectural picture. This is the real ambition, I suspect, of the astute architectural sensibility and sensitivity of NaJa & deOstos, in their imagining of new roles that architecture might play today in discussion and debate about global modernization and the paradoxes of how it has and continues to transform local cultures of all kinds today, whether those of local inhabitants, indigenous peoples, or design professionals. NaJa & deOstos brings back the idea that architecture—and moreover, architectural design—can operate as a form of cultural speculation. To do so is to see architecture as more than a discipline but as a unique kind of language that not only builds and inhabits our world but also its imagination and desire.

Brett Steele
London, April 2008

Introduction

*And what confronted him, instead of the darkness he
had expected, bewildered him completely. Everything was
still the same, exactly as he had found it on opening the
door the previous evening. The files of old papers and the
ink-bottles were still tumbled behind the threshold, the
Whipper with his rod and the warders with all their clothes
on were still standing there.*

—Franz Kafka, *The Trial*

Accounts of architectural inspiration originating largely
from nature and contained within sublime explorations
of its inner mathematical codes punctuate recent histo-
ries of architecture as much as more-ancient narratives.
Although formally attractive, the application of these
naturalistic sources is largely self-referential and focuses
on technical dexterities rather than any obvious invest-
ment in understanding and exploring the political forces
that shape not only people's lives but also architecture's
goals and fields of action. Those forces—the relationship
between individuals and institutions—and their social
and cultural implications are the starting point for our
projects. In other words, rather than focusing only on
technique, our architectural interests reside precisely in
the spatial investigation of individual, state, corporate, or
military relationships and how they can abruptly shift
individual and communal life stories, seemingly without
their consent. In order to manifest these complex situations, we explore architecture as a territory where the
absurd and contradictory aspects of the situations themselves can be identified within the resulting projects.

In our relatively short careers, we have discovered in
literary—as opposed to naturalistic—models a fertile
ground in which to investigate architecture as an interdis-
ciplinary language. It is a language that not only expresses
itself through the extremes of pragmatism or scientific

allegory but also one that can negotiate the threshold
between matter-of-fact reality and mysterious spatial
happenings.

We can trace our interest in exploring architecture
through literature to works such as Kafka's *The Trial*. This
book not only describes oppressive and alienating insti-
tutional forces but also depicts how these same forces
manifest themselves: elusive, absurd, and violent. For
example, the description of the warders' punishment
at the hands of the leather-clad Whipper in the lumber
room of a bank mutates a recognizable (and initially mun-
dane) environment into something sinister and ambiguous. Spatial and literary deformations and the blending of
parallel realities explored by Kafka and other authors like
Gabriel García Márquez and Jorge Luis Borges are the
operative inspiration for the greater part of our design processes. Specifically, we are interested in investigating spatial
design through opposing elements, cultural nuances
presented in ideas and issues usually considered outside the scope of our profession. The resulting architecture can be characterized as *ambiguous space* in which
ambivalence presides and discordant logics are mani-
fested. These places do not offer solutions but stimulate
a constant questioning about architectural ideas and our
own role as creators in an irresolute and often contradictory discipline.

The Trial reveals that what seems a strange depiction
of reality is actually a much more sophisticated, darker
excursion into the nuances of juxtaposed logics and
worlds. The fissures opened by Kafka's twisted unreal-
ity are utterly fascinating. By articulating our own projects through a similarly uncanny but subtle set of spatial
arrangements, we approach architecture as an open
language—and one that can address issues once considered unsuitable to its *status quo*. Based on this literary, novelistic appropriation, our own architectural path

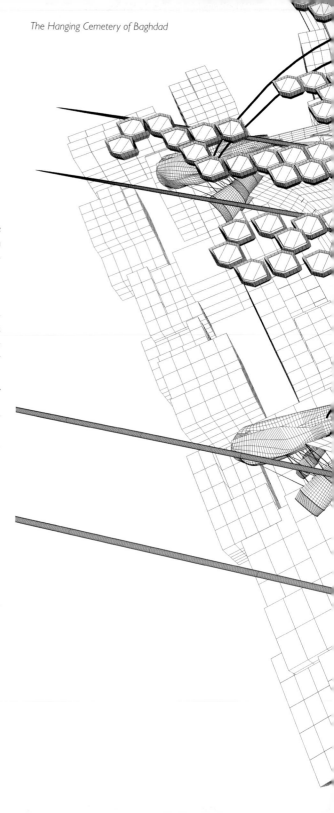

has been guided by the exploration of those strange elements—the common fissures that exist between oppressed individuals/communities and powerful political forces.

Though long established in theoretical and historical debates, the concept of treating architecture as a language—communicating and materializing spatial ideas—is paramount when reflecting on the practice of architecture today. The logic of global commercialization has largely privileged conventional architectural models, resulting in a straightforward dialogue of traditionally accepted ideas. Far from promoting arcane essentialist views on pure architectural language, crossbreeding architecture—exploring its boundaries rather than its center—generates a fresh set of architectural possibilities. Design via literary models, such as Kafkaesque scenarios or the techniques of magical realism, opens up a new arena for addressing the complex political issues inherent in every project and empowers us to explore relevant contemporary issues otherwise ignored in mainstream architecture. To paraphrase Sartre, this incursion into a parallel expression of architectural language enables us to "become situated" within the world, responding directly to the things around us rather than being ineffective spectators. There are many ways to be involved with world events, both as professionals and citizens; for us, literature inspires a broad spectrum of engagements.

The nature of the relationship between the subject and this method of investigation demands flexibility. In the absurd and unexpected imaginations of writers of fiction, we find a compelling inspiration to celebrate that freedom. Highly unlikely starting points for architecture—for example, examinations of tempestuous subjects like wars, the use and reuse of nuclear power plants, or the infrastructural consequences involved in the construction of large dams—allow for poetic license, and the

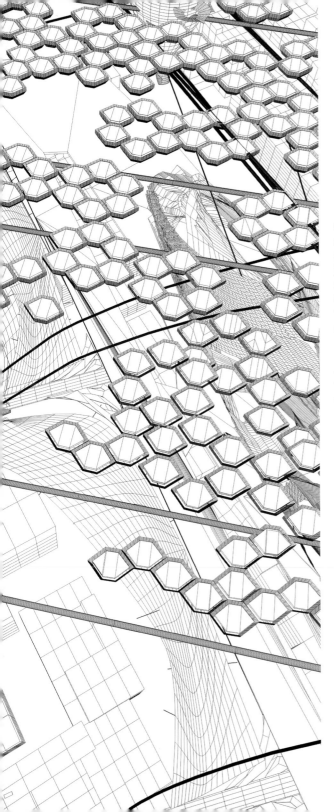

supplementary literary tools of extreme irony, sarcasm, and humor forced us to test our own design ideas. Just as there exists a diverse array of writerly genres—from journalistic essays to poetry and short stories—there are multiple modes of output for architectural work. In this sense, this conceptual experimentation of form, presentation, and spatial organization suggests not so much a manifesto as a more continuous form of research, striving always for new forms of expression.

Absorbing literary and rhetorical devices into architectural projects has generated hybrid results in which the end design no longer possesses a single primary purpose. Central to this hybridization is that the spatial script of how a politically engaged building discourse should operate has lost its philanthropic or altruistic role. These projects not only fulfill a program or propose solutions but also materialize conflicting stories, framing events into a plot—magical, ironic, tragic, or informative. To remove space from its familiar function is to open it up to interpretation for viewers, users, or readers and to detach its investigation from any messianic connotations. The resulting enigmatic spaces, where opposite logics coexist and where obscure meanings appear, turn interpretation into the paramount architectural experience. Ambiguous spaces are not the product of another normative architectural manifesto or paradigm but are reactionary design experiments in inquisitive architecture that is a product of its time.

A fundamental aspect of storytelling is the bond created between writer and subject. Often, stories allow the writer to recount the tales of those who have not had the chance to tell their own. This key separation between the subject of a story and the writer's perspective can define and position a book in its own specific time and place. For example, the stories of the South African apartheid years are now told, in large, by a collective of white South

African writers (notably, writers such as J. M. Coetzee) or Kafka, who wrote his novel *Amerika* without ever having traveled overseas. The nature of this type of literary engagement ratifies unexpected relationships and different points of view.

The first of our projects, *The Hanging Cemetery of Baghdad*, derived precisely from this premise. Though geographically and ethnically removed from Iraq and its people, we, like many others, felt sympathetic to the suffering portrayed on television, the internet, and in newspapers since the Coalition forces' invasion of the country in 2003. Suddenly, being conscious of the separation between spectator and actual events meant being situated, mediated by both passivity and contempt and significant enough to discuss through design. The absence of a client and a design brief was rebalanced by the importance of the task and the opportunity to express our own stories, thoughts, and feelings. We used this geographical distance and mediated experience to define the project's concept, critical perspective, and research focus. During project development we found curious reports and articles related to the ancient history of the area. The only records of certain events, monuments, and buildings—including the Hanging Gardens of Babylon—came from dubious information and unreliable historical documents.

This enigmatic historical panorama paralleled our own mediated position: as distanced spectators, following an edited, broadcast war in London and receiving disputable statistics. When an architect chooses a design, he or she also inevitably projects a specific image. Architects, in this sense, constantly situate themselves as actors, participants, and players. Unfortunately, factors like geographic distance are rarely used as design tools (despite the fact that many students and architects treat international competitions and commissions in diverse parts of the globe as local enterprises). In contrast, *The Hanging Cemetery of Baghdad*

was heavily rooted in and shaped by our own position as authors living in London and discussing the city of Baghdad—with the project design based on camera positions, angles, and broadcast time frames.

We have already discussed the importance of reevaluating the architect's position on polemical subjects and applying it as a tool for design via auxiliary literary devices. But is the designed object the main aspiration of this personal process? Although we have described ambiguous spaces as the end result, our ambitions are not limited to this. The programs of our ambiguous spaces derive from specific research and critical positioning. This critical angle shifts the focus away from the final object, toward the actual design process. Consequently, in designing those spaces we have been consistently influenced by the specifics of the project's location—studying fields and angles complementary to the explicit problem at hand such as nuclear reactions or huge dam operations and impacts. From creating landscape by simulated nuclear explosions to defining anthropomorphic building programs, an open design process has been our only constant. But the open-endedness of architectural projects without external parameters has its own implicit challenges—how can design question social and political conditions without resorting to the same old answers, the same old building programs?

In his seminal early books Rem Koolhaas investigated these themes and proposed, instead of buildings with singular functions, alternative narratives, cross-programming, and scripts for the city. We share a similar conceptual interest in spatial scripts that expose the absurdities and contradictions in inhabiting hostile, polemic, or suspiciously familiar environments.

Scripts, in this sense, organize spaces, implications, and narratives. Plots such as the one within Kafka's *The*

Trial illustrate how a chain of causality between absurd happenings and surreal events can create an influence beyond its own references and context; the story is not a mere allegory. Since Kafka's intent was to write fiction, the aesthetic qualities of the book acquire autonomy and validation. Our projects are not scientific reports or novels but an investigative architecture inspired by both. Using this condition we have consistently pushed the literal elements of architecture to literary extremes—such as territories of cause and effect, constructability, and structural equilibrium. We made design decisions not in pursuit of originality so much as out of the necessity for an additive imagination, one able to incorporate invisible and tactile references.

Our fundamental role as architects is to promote challenging programs that encourage questioning and discovery and to create projects (built or unbuilt) that confront our daily routine, that demand to be explored. Exquisite atmospheres composed alongside uncertainty or ambiguity of spaces can unveil experiences and adventures. Working from this assumption, one of our recent projects, *The Pregnant Island*, investigates the impact of large dams on communities in China and Brazil. Inspired by heartbreaking statistics about gender inequality, mass migration, and the loss of culture and a desire to explore the subject outside the problem-solving straitjacket, we try to design not only from spreadsheets and numerical information, but also from mythical and magical stories.

Dams supply energy and control floods and irrigation but have also dislocated up to eighty million people worldwide and have precipitated irrevocable environmental damage. Rather than judging the technical merits of the dam (something beyond our capabilities), we chose to tell a story via design about the people who once inhabited those pre-dam landscapes. Influenced by local native fertility myths and South American magical-realist authors

like Gabriel García Márquez, Jorge Luis Borges, and Alejo Carpentier, we felt that a fictional entity alongside a quasi-tangible building could capture the magnitude and complexity of what we had discovered. (For example, some 1,600 hilltops were turned into an archipelago of islands during the strategic flooding of the 1,100-square-mile Brazilian Tucuruí Dam reservoir.) Our concept of a pregnant island is not just a surrealist imposition, but derives from native tales. The references for defining the island parameters—kinetic movements, growth, and relation to the water tide—were not only derived locally but also from fictional stories such as Jonathan Swift's *Gulliver's Travels* and Daniel Defoe's *Robinson Crusoe*. Distinct from satirical geographies, like Gulliver's flying island, Laputa, or even the island of Tool from Rabelais's *Gargantua and Pantagruel*, where the narrative is unmistakably allegorical, we conceived this ambiguous concept as a design piece with layered spatial qualities rather than as a one-dimensional message.

An earlier project, *Nuclear Breeding*, explores similar issues of the impact of technology on a unique locale. *Nuclear Breeding* explores the ambiguous story of Orford Ness, a former nuclear test site in England. The first British atomic bomb, the Blue Danube, was tested here but ultimately detonated in Australia, with catastrophic consequences for the native population. The project investigates craters by simulating explosions on the Orford Ness site. The design utilizes the idea of chain reaction and other misuses of nuclear simulations to generate a landscape design and erect dwelling compartments.

With the projects illustrated in this publication, we hope to share our findings and design research. Through them, ambiguity becomes a creative instrument, a fierce and engaged spatial stance, a device that can be expressed not only pragmatically but also ironically.

Orford Ness
Southeast coast of England

Nuclear Breeding

But Africa. They had simply let their enthusiasm get the
better of them, and you had to admire that, although m
thoughtful advice would have cautioned them to perhap
let it wait a bit until, for instance, Project Farmland had
been completed. Now there the Nazis had shown geniu
the artist in them had truly emerged. The Mediterranea
Sea bottled up, drained, made into tillable farmland,
through the use of atomic power—what daring! How th
sniggerers had been set back on their heels, for instance
certain scoffing merchants along Montgomery Street. An
as a matter of fact, Africa had almost been successful.

—Philip K. Dick, *The Man in the High Castle*

Today the former nuclear test site
houses a nature reserve.

Ambiguous seems to be the best word to
describe the history of Orford Ness, a former nuclear
test facility located in southeast England. Once a military
site used to launch reconnaissance sorties, experiment
with aerial photography, develop a radar system, and test
ballistics for the Blue Danube (the first British atomic
bomb in the 1950s), it now houses a nature reserve.
The Blue Danube, the most destructive of Orford Ness's
military legacy, was not detonated on English soil but in
Maralinga, Australia. According to Australian newspaper
reports, the local population suffered from the impact of
the radioactive clouds resulting from negligent preven-
tive measures by the governments involved. This veiled
relationship between the two distinct geographies of
Orford Ness and Maralinga was the beginning of our
Nuclear Breeding project.

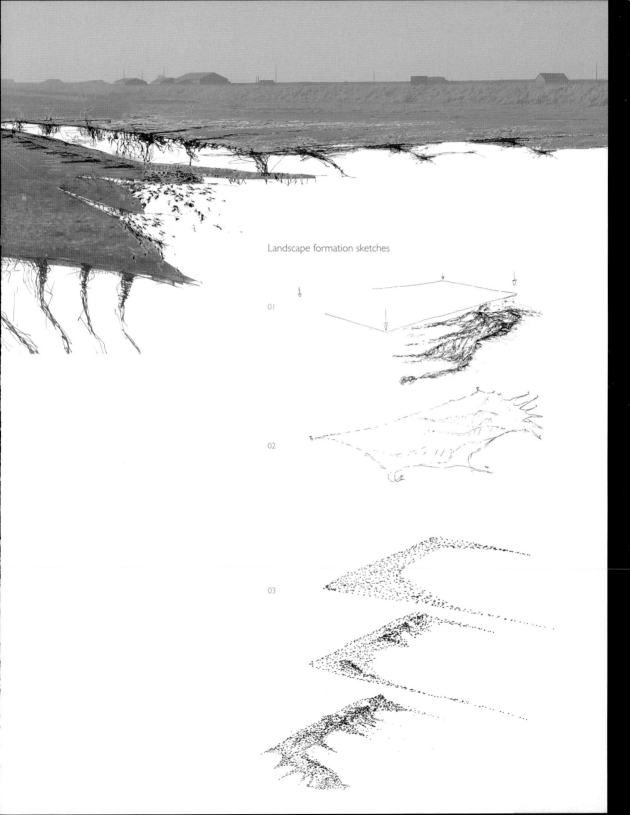

Landscape formation sketches

01

02

03

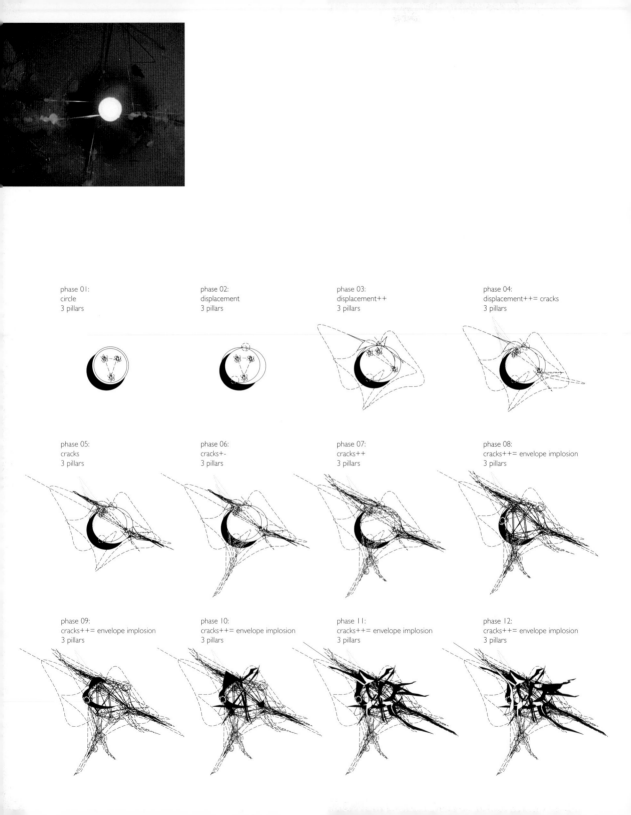

phase 01:
circle
3 pillars

phase 02:
displacement
3 pillars

phase 03:
displacement++
3 pillars

phase 04:
displacement++= cracks
3 pillars

phase 05:
cracks
3 pillars

phase 06:
cracks+-
3 pillars

phase 07:
cracks++
3 pillars

phase 08:
cracks++= envelope implosion
3 pillars

phase 09:
cracks++= envelope implosion
3 pillars

phase 10:
cracks++= envelope implosion
3 pillars

phase 11:
cracks++= envelope implosion
3 pillars

phase 12:
cracks++= envelope implosion
3 pillars

The first step was to plot a story that would encompass the complexity of the history and subject as well as inform the design process. In this sense we used narrative as a selective and generative tool—*generative* meaning having the power to originate design investigations—to explore the form-finding process with a certain freedom and trust in the fertility of the subject matter.

Nuclear Breeding explores the mechanisms of the nuclear bomb itself. We observed via online videos atomic explosions carried out in places like Bikini Atoll in the Marshall Islands and the Nevada test site in the United States and mapped the physical effects of nuclear detonation on land and water. The resulting large, deep, rounded craters possessed distinct sizes and shapes depending on the power of the detonated bomb. We studied each crater in order to understand this extreme "landscaping technique."

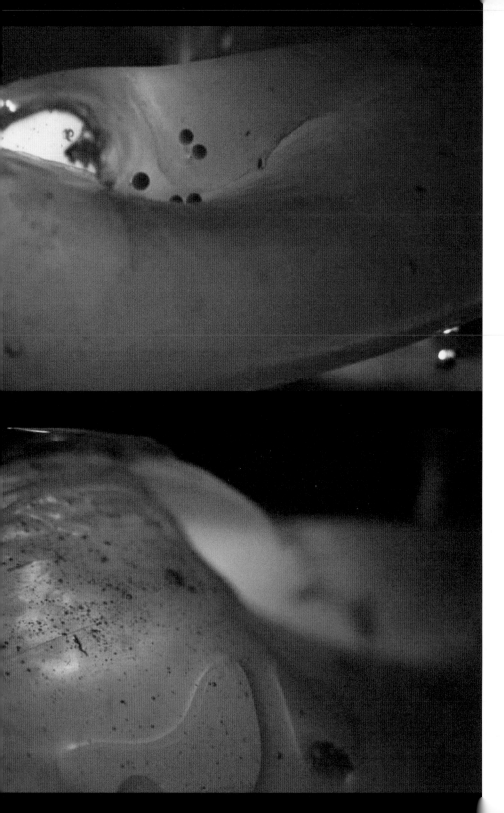

To mimic this megalomaniacal earth-moving, we made a series of drawings that simulated nuclear explosions, impacts, and potential soil cracks. Our main goal was to investigate generating a landscape design via fictional computer-simulated explosions. This form-finding method was divided into three parts: creating formal three-dimensional diagrams through computer drawings, then mapping, inserting design decisions in the process. After studying our initial computer-generated diagrams we investigated spatial arrangements in the second design phase via hand drawings.

For us, computer-generated drawings have always been part of the process but never the final answer. To map and assign functions for the crater diagrams with hand drawings was to insert human scale and intimacy into the material. Taking into consideration parameters such as water proximity and shingle beaches terrain (in order to elaborate on the generated craters' depth, width, and soil structure), we determined the orientation and specifics of this landscape design. We mapped recurring typologies of craters and separated them into clusters based on their similarities—length, depth, form, and potentials (such as routes, contained spaces). We also created fictional characters, users that could interact with the space, to determine the craters' primary and secondary uses.

Chain-reaction device experiments using dry CO_2, wax, latex skin, and motors

Shingle area in Orford Ness.
Used for testing Blue Danube,
the first British atomic bomb.

Vegetation area between river
and shingle region.

The beginning and the end of a
visible green zone.

But there's something beyond…

The resulting referential and sometimes metaphoric characters were introduced and set against architecture's typically vague interest in personalized spaces. This resulted in different programs to fit each user's personality.

The first group lives in one cluster west
of the shingle area (an area full of small
rounded pebbles).

The cluster is placed there because of wind
direction. Having developed parachutelike
devices, the inhabitants can fly until they
reach seaside.

0.1 WIND + flying

01 Cluster 0.1 is inhabited by young individuals. A mix of
feelings, including impulsion, excitement, disappointment,
and melancholy dominates the place.

02 The characters of cluster 0.2 grow crops on large fields.
Their space is oriented toward a lighthouse located at the
southeast of the shingle area of Orford Ness.

03 Cluster 0.3 hosts individuals located at the center of
cultivation fields. Rainwater is collected in containers and
used for irrigation.

04 Cluster 0.4 includes pneumatic structures and platforms
on the seaside.

The inhabitants of this cluster live in separate craters and develop structures to expand their fields.

They drag water from the river and develop irrigation systems, and their boundaries always grow.

0.2 RIVER + vegetation

Area filled with vegetation. Used for military tests during the First and Second World Wars.

River located across the site maintaining the existing vegetation on-site

0.4 SEA + nostalgia

The fourth group lives near the sea at the shingle area. They inhabit pneumatic devices that are connected to platforms placed in the sea.

Water is pumped from the sea to the pneumatic structures, generating a dynamic space.

0.3 RAIN + visibility

The world is still spinning.

Group three lives deep inside the craters.

The inhabitants collect rainwater for agricultural use and have their bodies hung on low-tech capsules inherited from atomic equipment left on-site.

The site of Orford Ness was used as a test area by the British Army.

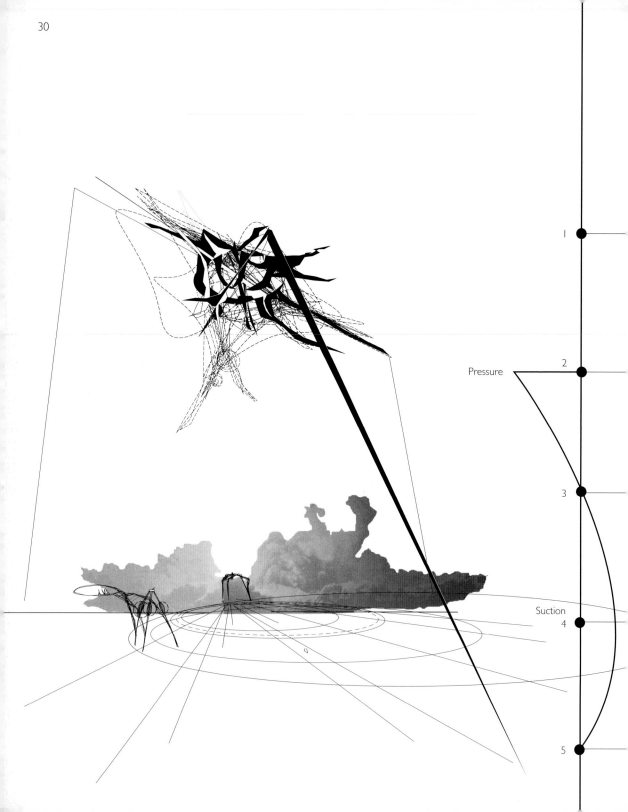

Pressure

Suction

1

2

3

4

5

Variations of blast effects associated with
positive and negative phases depending
on pressure and time

31

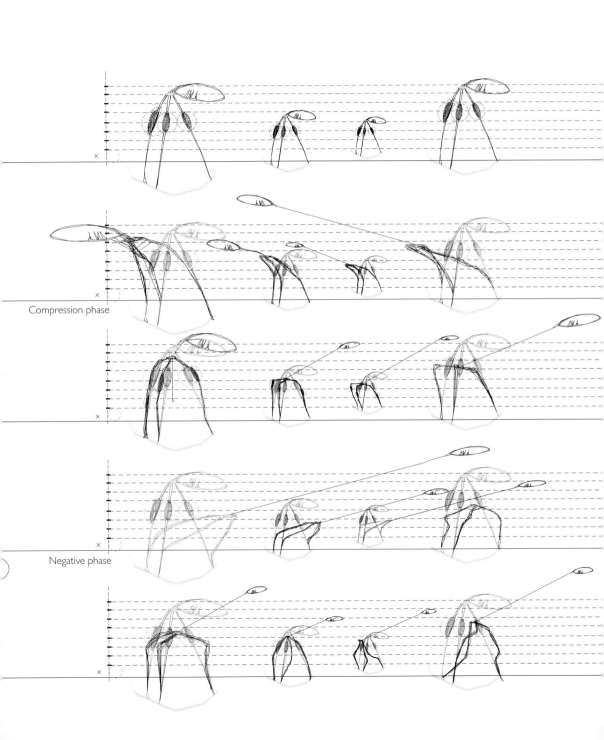

Compression phase

Negative phase

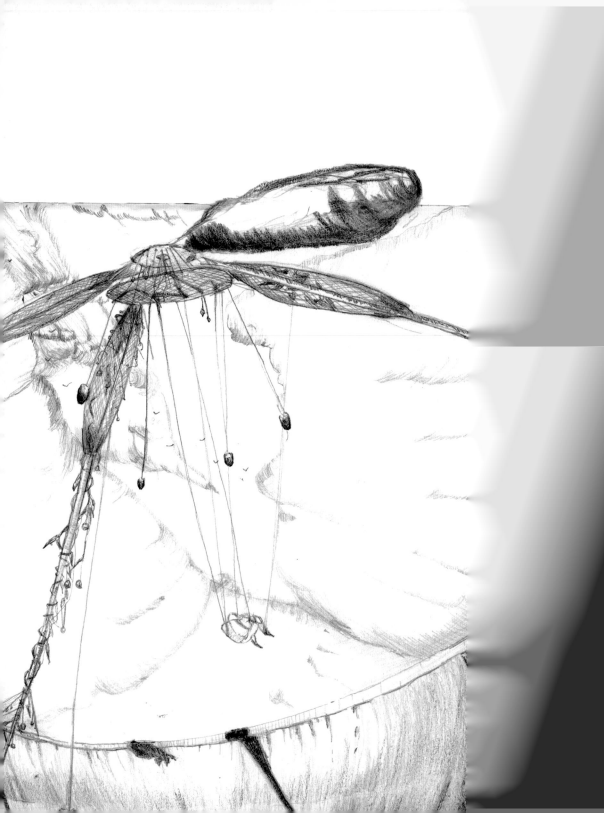

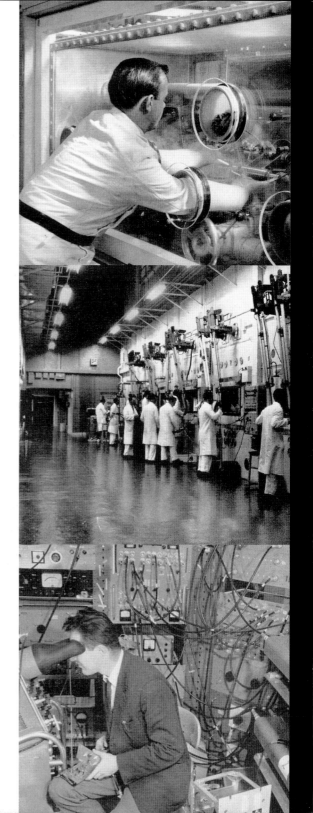

The Master-Slave device enables scientists to handle radioactive materials. From J. F. Munce, *The Architect in the Nuclear Age: Design of Buildings to House Radioactivity* (London: Iliffe Books, 1964).

As in Project Farmland in Philip K. Dick's *The Man in the High Castle*, the destructive power of atomic bombs to generate an alternative life model—as highlighted in this chapter's epigraph—resonates with the contradictory nature of the military use of such technology, i.e., creating farmland from the use of atomic power! However, the Orford Ness farmed craters and landscape experiment in the *Nuclear Breeding* project do not celebrate technology as satirized by Dick but the possible alternative outcomes of the same technologies.

In order to explore the farming potential of the designed craters, we generated mechanical equipment. For example, we proposed an irrigation device called Master-Slave based on the handling machines scientists use to manipulate nuclear substances from a distance. The original device consists of responsive mechanical arms that enable the scientists to control contaminated environments without being directly connected to it. This design enables a single control unit—the user—to manipulate multiple irrigation arms. To investigate additional formal and expressive configurations, we submitted the modified Master-Slave machine to a simulated nuclear-blast effect. All blast effects create positive- and negative-pressures phases, with high-velocity wind traveling first outward and then immediately reversing back toward the zero point. The results were clumsy, finicky structures. Placed on the top of the craters, they can be used first as mobile irrigation arms and second as customized plug-in kits, as inhabitants transform the arms themselves into short-stay dwelling capsules.

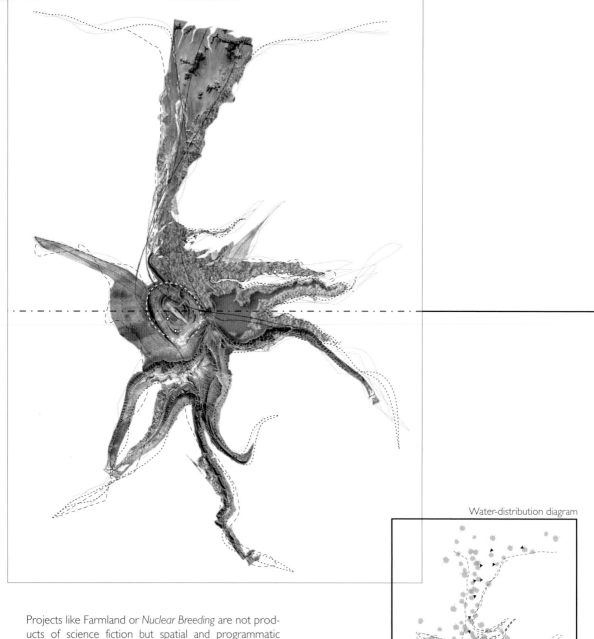

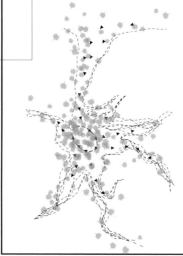

Water-distribution diagram

Projects like Farmland or *Nuclear Breeding* are not products of science fiction but spatial and programmatic investigations into the mysterious field of military nuclear technology. The fictional platform integral to both projects opens up fissures that allow for a kind of tantalized examination. Alongside more pragmatic solutions, however, the landscape, mechanical devices, and spatial organization generated here are ineffectual. Nonetheless, they compose a scene of memory and production, nostalgia and invention, which bind remembrance of the past to the necessity of progress.

Vegetation-field diagram

01 Rainwater collection

02 Storage

03 Distribution

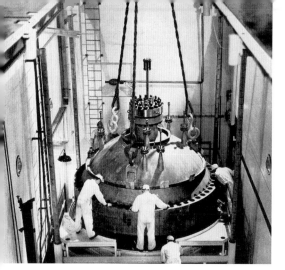

Bomb handling. From Munce, *The Architect in the Nuclear Age*.

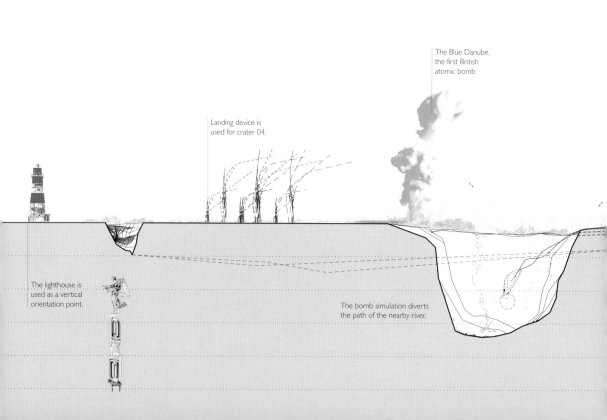

The Blue Danube, the first British atomic bomb

Landing device is used for crater 04.

The lighthouse is used as a vertical orientation point.

The bomb simulation diverts the path of the nearby river.

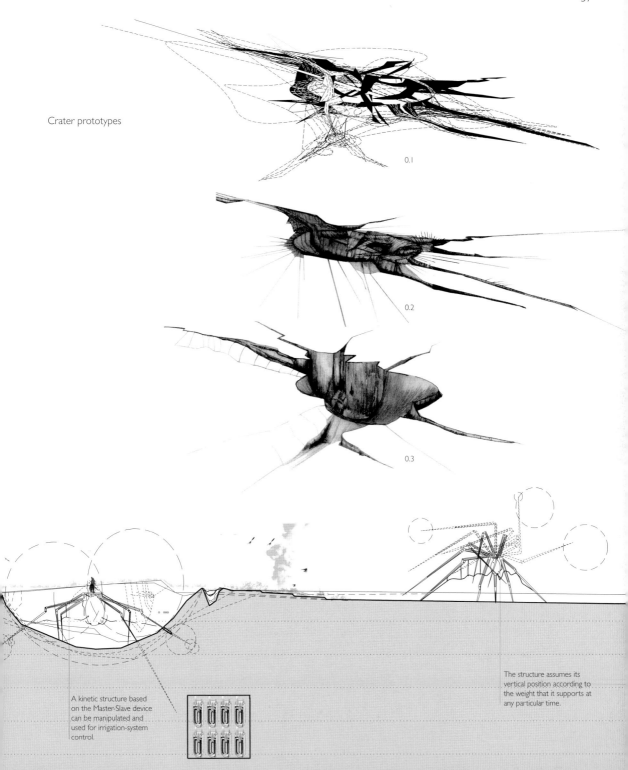

Crater prototypes

0.1

0.2

0.3

A kinetic structure based on the Master-Slave device can be manipulated and used for irrigation-system control.

The structure assumes its vertical position according to the weight that it supports at any particular time.

Tucuruí Reservoir
Brazilian Amazon, 2006
Photograph by Eneida Castro

The Pregnant Island

Father Nicanor tried to impress the military authorities with the miracle of levitation and had his head split open by the butt of a soldier's rifle....

Not only was he as heavy as ever, but during his prolonged stay under the chestnut tree he had developed the faculty of being able to increase his weight at will, to such a degree that seven men were unable to lift him and they had to drag him to the bed.

—Gabriel García Márquez, *One Hundred Years of Solitude*

Magical Realism

Macondo, a fictional town created by Gabriel García Márquez in *One Hundred Years of Solitude*, is a place of binary extremes. On the one hand, magical events punctuate the narrative of the book—things that defy scientific reality are depicted as matter-of-fact happenings: shape-shifting, unusual life spans, and levitation. On the other hand, the book contains equally shocking but familiar human practices like exploitation and ruthless violence and the brutality of modernity and progress. Though the reader can easily distinguish between these extremes, they are presented with a singular authorial voice, and magical and factual events are equally perceived by the characters of García Márquez's book as components of the everyday.

This storytelling mechanism, magical realism, has similarities with other literary genres like surrealism and science

fiction, but is nevertheless formally distinct from its cousins. For example, the fantastic happenings that take place in Macondo are treated as everyday occurrences, but when the protagonist of Kafka's *The Metamorphosis*, Gregor Samsa, is transformed into an "insect," his family reacts with awe and horror. This commonplace treatment of the supernatural in Macondo grounds the book's narrative tone in a strange but recognizable reality. By controlling the magical elements, the author foregrounds other issues—like social exploitation and political dilemmas.

As discussed by many literary critics and readers, Macondo not only represents the historical struggle of South America against postcolonial forces and provincial corruption but also the ascension of indigenous traditions, such as storytelling and native myths, that help maintain the supernatural and the mystical in people's lives across Latin America.

View from the top of the Tucuruí Dam wall looking toward the spillway (downstream)

In the mid-1980s the giant Tucuruí Dam
was built on the lower Tocantins River in the
Brazilian Amazon. It is the largest dam ever
built in a tropical rain forest and the fifth-largest
hydroelectric power station in the world.

Opposite: The Three Gorges Dam on the
Yangtze River in China will be completed in
2009 and begin operation in 2011. It will be
the largest hydroelectric power station in the
world by capacity, supplying one-ninth of China's
electricity. Three Gorges Dam, NASA/GSFC/
METI/ERSDAC/JAROS, and U.S./Japan ASTER
Science Team.

Dams

Our interest in researching the impact of large dams initially developed from our project for the second Istanbul Architecture Biennale on the theme of asphalt and water. Although the event was canceled due to sponsorship troubles, our awareness of dams' impact—and the broader relationship between infrastructures and cities worldwide—sparked the current project. After book and report research; overseas site visits; talks with involved parties—government institutions, developers, engineers, environmentalists, local communities, and international/local anti/pro dam organizations; hours of telephone conversations; and encountering impenetrable bureaucracy, we constructed a broad overview to begin the project.

The locals' narratives and their strong bond to specific natural features—rivers, plants, animals, geographies, forest sounds—and the community's imagination were pleasant discoveries and suggested the relationship between this project and magical realism. The inclusive nature of the literary genre—mixing magical/fictional and factual/historical events—made it a fecund tool to address the complex realities of the dam's subject. The intricate reality of building a dam is that factual/quantitative data—landownership, financial compensation, gender—must be balanced with magical/qualitative factors—creationist myths, local gods, ritual grounds. Based on this magical-factual narrative technique and our own agenda as architects, we explored the vast—both literally and symbolically—topic of dams. After our initial research, we focused on two particular examples, the Three Gorges Dam in Sandouping, China, and the Tucuruí Dam in Pará, Brazil.

Large dams generate hydroelectric power, supply water, and control irrigation, and provide an energy resource hailed as clean. However, large dams also have less laudable impacts, including technical and financial shortcomings (unachieved targets on power generation and irrigation and cost overruns); damaging effects on local ecosystems (loss of forestation, wildlife habitats, aquatic biodiversity, and water quality); and, a more immediate problem, the displacement of vast numbers of people. According to the World Commission on Dams (WCD), "some 40 to 80 million people have been physically displaced by dams worldwide." The majority of this population has not been compensated, with indigenous or vulnerable ethic minorities suffering "disproportionate levels of displacement and negative impacts on livelihood, culture, and spiritual existence."[1]

In a survey of 125 dams initiated in order to "generate broader patterns and trends," WCD learned of gender gaps—women had suffered higher social costs. At both of the dams we investigated recurring tragedies: ineffective displacement patterns caused a broken sense of community and a loss of livelihood, which in turn precipitated rises in alcohol abuse, domestic violence, suicides, and sexually transmitted diseases and a decrease in fertility rates. Entire cities have turned into ghost towns and ancient archaeological sites flooded. These types of reports are utterly devastating.

[1] World Commission on Dams, *Dams and Development: A New Framework for Decision-Making* (London: Earthscan Publications, 2000), 104.

2000

2006

One-third of the countries in the world rely on hydropower. Large dams generate 19 percent of the world's electricity.

One-half of the world's large dams were built for irrigation. Thirty to forty percent of the 271 Mio hectares irrigated worldwide rely on dams.

Dams have led to significant and irreversible loss of species and ecosystems.

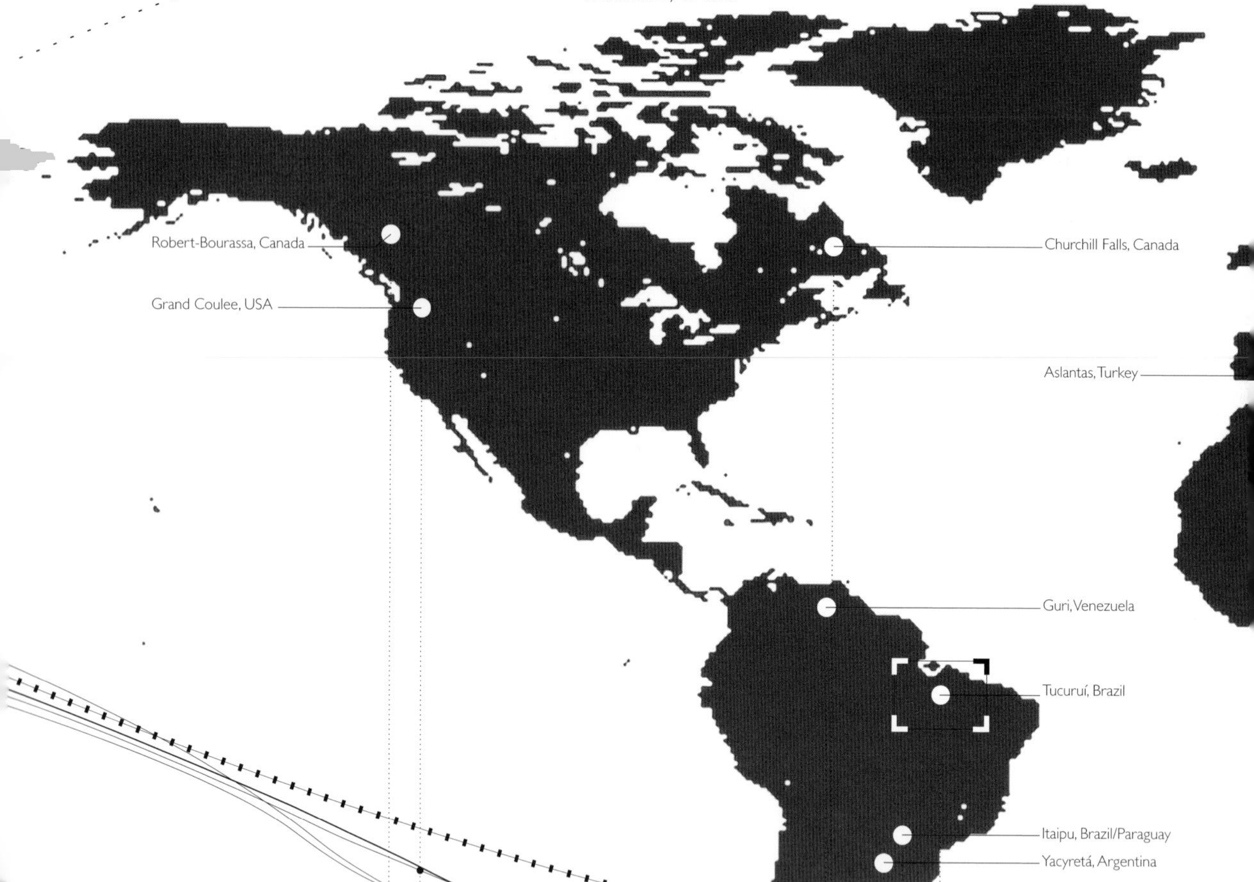

Robert-Bourassa, Canada

Grand Coulee, USA

Churchill Falls, Canada

Aslantas, Turkey

Guri, Venezuela

Tucuruí, Brazil

Itaipu, Brazil/Paraguay

Yacyretá, Argentina

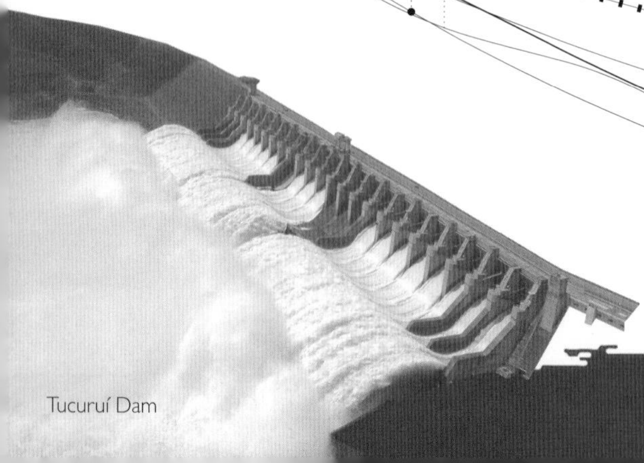

Tucuruí Dam

With the construction of the Ilisu Dam, the ancient city of Hasankeyf in Turkey will be lost.

Forty to eighty Mio people have been physically displaced worldwide.

The Three Gorges Dam on the Yangtze River in China is the largest water-conservation project in the world.

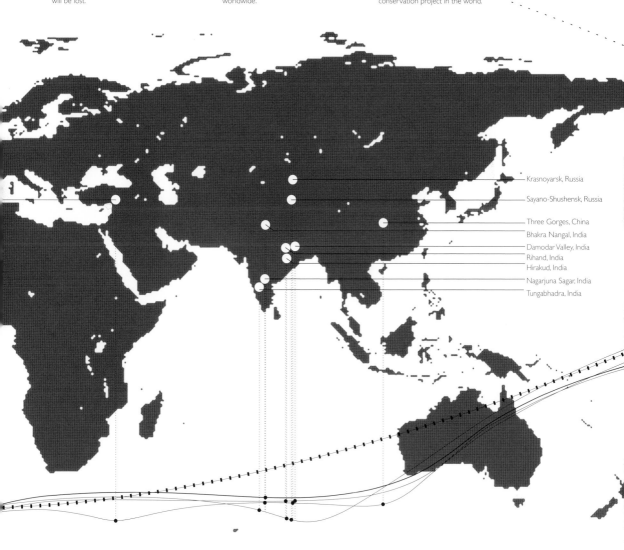

Krasnoyarsk, Russia

Sayano-Shushensk, Russia

Three Gorges, China
Bhakra Nangal, India
Damodar Valley, India
Rihand, India
Hirakud, India
Nagarjuna Sagar, India
Tungabhadra, India

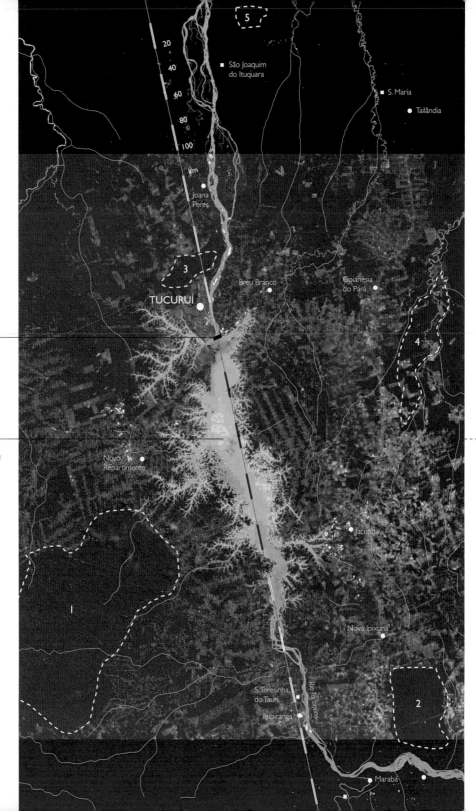

Tucuruí Dam

hydroelectric dam
completed in 1984
length: 4.3 miles
height: 256 feet

Dam Reservoir

flooded area: 1,110 mi²
total volume: 10.9 mi³
useful volume: 7.7 mi³
max. length: 106 miles
max. width: 25 miles
depth: 243 feet

Indigenous societies in
the dam region:

1 PARAKANA
   relocated and split up
   several times

2 GAVIAO DA
   MONTANHA
   persuaded to move to
   Mae Maria Indigenous
   Land

3 TROCARA
   relocated downstream

4 AMAGANES

5 ANAMBE

Greater London

610 mi²

inundation/flood ⟶ permanent wetlands ⟶ submerged rotting ⟶ loss of tropical
                                                vegetation   rainforest cover

resettlement of 14,000   mosquito plagues   increased toxicity and   change in rainfall
people formerly   general contamination   patterns and
residing in the dam-   increase in the number   distribution
reservoir area   of malaria cases   greenhouse gases

displacement of 250   diseases   chemical changes in   alteration of regional
km of roads   the water downstream,   climate
                                                   drop in water quality
relocation of 280,000   global climate change
animals   high fish mortality
                                                   rates, reduction of fish
loss of historic   species
archaeological sites
                                                   reduction in fisheries,
loss of arable land   drop in fish supply

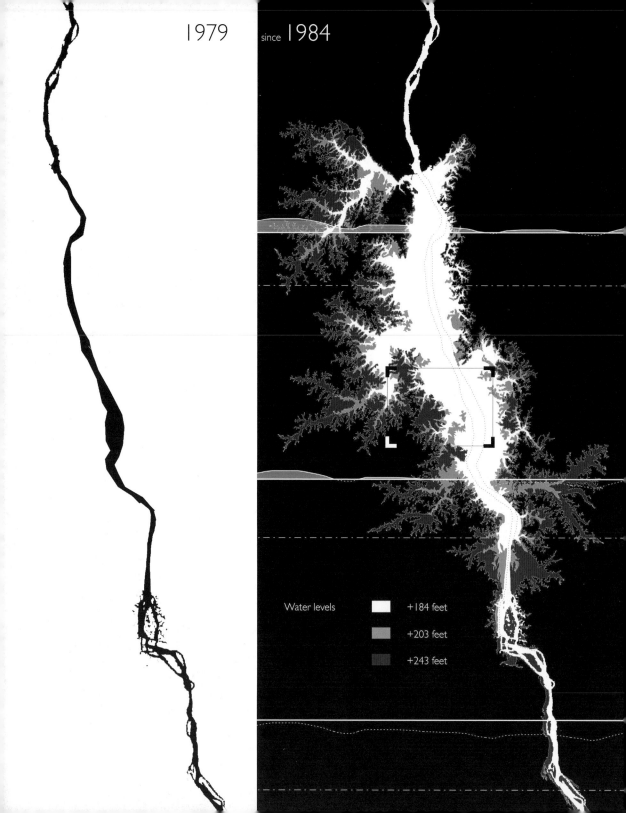

1979   since 1984

Water levels

+184 feet

+203 feet

+243 feet

Diagrams showing water versus land territory in the dam reservoir. Former hilltops transform into a myriad of islands.

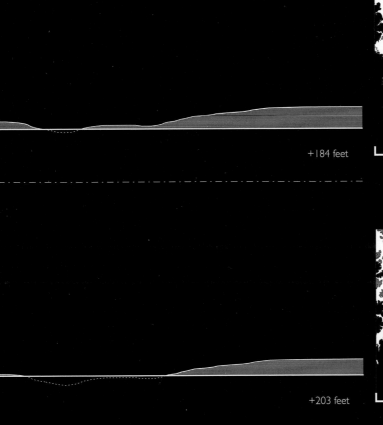

+184 feet

+203 feet

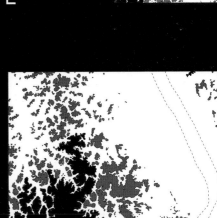

+243 feet

The Pregnant Island

Overview

As in the *Nuclear Breeding* and *Hanging Cemetery* projects, we created a narrative that could absorb the dichotomies within the data we gathered. We designed the landscape based on the two facts that sound fictional: that 1,600 hilltops were transformed into islands by the initial flooding of the Tucuruí Dam reservoir and that the water level can vary by sixty feet between wet and dry seasons, mutating the landscape from valley to lake. The inspirations for generating a partially kinetic island were native fertility tales (particularly their belief that nature is a living entity, with deities impersonating landscape features); native creation myths; and our own associations with the term *Mother Earth* (a parochial term but one that has a universal resonance).

The Concept

The proposed anthropomorphic terrain is embedded with seriousness and humor in equal measures. Comparing Amazonian tribes' perception of nature with the idealized mainstream Occidental vision opened provocative design opportunities. For the former, nature is a living entity, generous but hostile; for the latter, the anthropomorphizing of nature into a nurturing Gaia is a metaphoric and poetic device. The former believes in invisible supernatural powers; the latter in a clear separation between real and unreal, factual and imaginary, science and myth.

We explored this dichotomy through speculation, what Jorge Luis Borges called the "invention of circumstances," a sort of "what if." What if both universes, magical and scientific, could merge? The meeting of the two parallel worlds would mirror the dam's own condition—a colossal piece of engineering placed in archaeological grounds among Amazonian rituals. Equally important to our process were literary works by writers such as Gabriel García Márquez, Salman Rushdie, and Alejo Carpentier. The way these texts incorporate fantastical happenings to heighten their narration of class struggles was very inspiring. We did not seek to mimic their unique and sophisticated narratives but to investigate how their abnormal narratives generated compelling pictures of complex situations.

"Behold, a virgin shall conceive."
—Isaiah 7:14

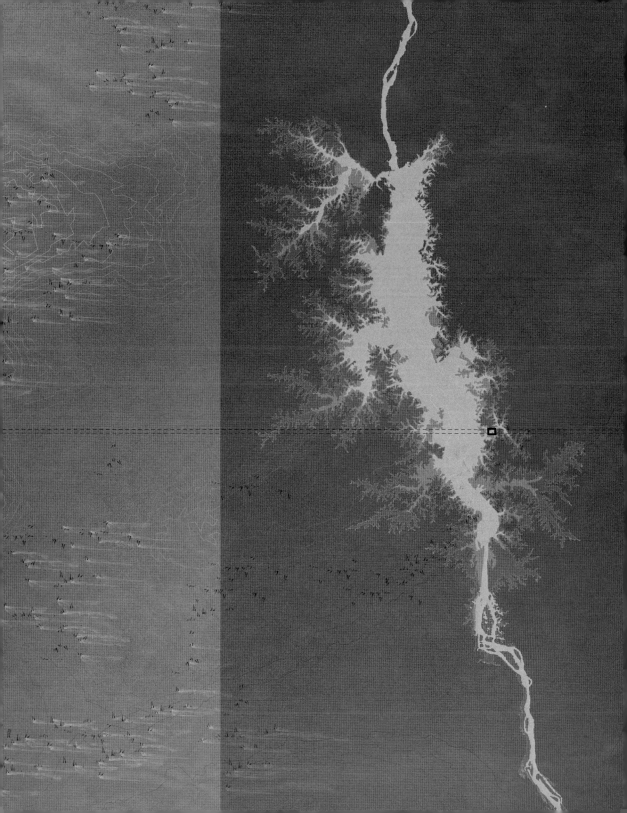

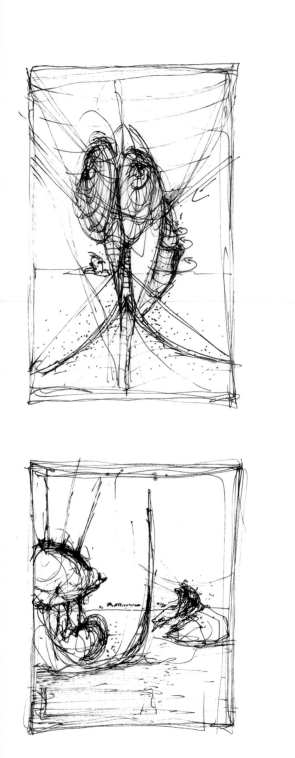
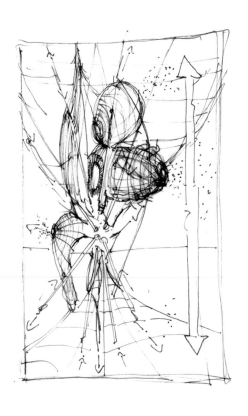

Conceptual sketches of the *maloca*
showing inside-outside relationships

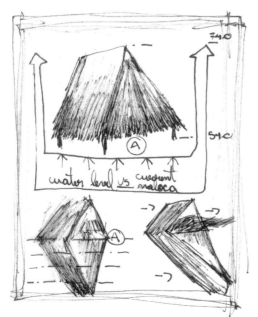

Distinct from Macondo and its seven generations of family life, our conceptual island evolved with only one generation of characters. The design process was divided into three parts: the island, a dwelling building, and the area between them. Having studied the landscape pre-dam and after the construction of Tucuruí, we derived a series of parameters to define how the building envelope and the island's pregnancy—its kinetic aspects—would interact. Since the situation of a pregnant island is our invention, a few conditions of pregnancy had to be translated: from the gestation of a female animal to the "carrying of" the anthropomorphic island; from distended (swollen) parts and fatigue (slow transformations), weight gain, and center of gravity shift to the invisible aspects of gestation, sensitiveness to the surrounding environment, birth, and possible miscarriage.

We then mapped and zoned the island according to areas where swellings might erupt and where more stable geological areas would allow for a building footprint. The concept of the pregnant island was not simply an allegorical addition or a metaphor but a key design-process tool—one that did not use digital and mechanical generative technologies as ends in themselves but as the amalgamation of rational (building structure) and irrational (the anthropomorphic island) designed elements.

Island formations

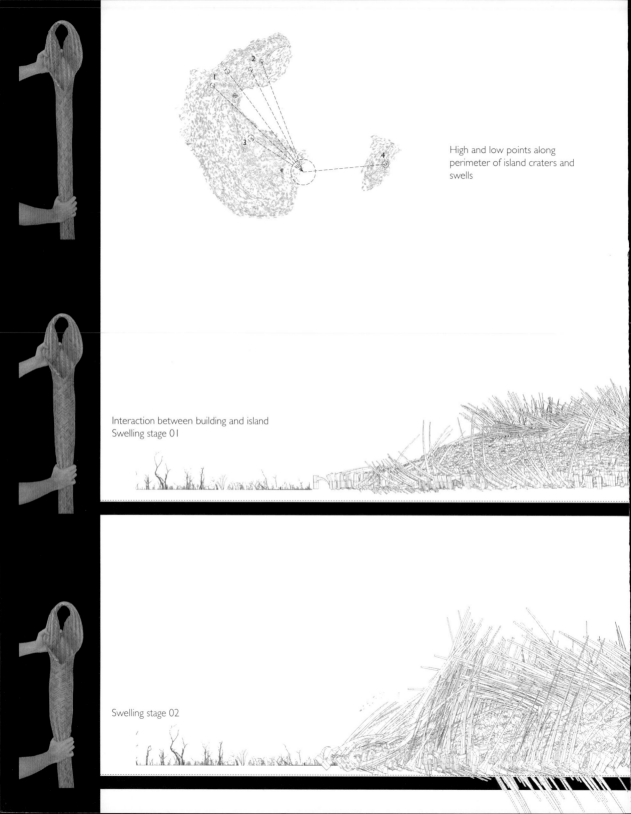

High and low points along
perimeter of island craters and
swells

Interaction between building and island
Swelling stage 01

Swelling stage 02

The Building—A *Maloca*

A reinvented version of the native Amazonizan communal house is located on the northeast part of the island.
The vegetation at this location has disappeared, and the
land is eroded due to the massive tide changes. The building serves as dwelling and includes typical elements of
the indigenous architecture arranged, atypically, around a
vertical axis. The sinuous curves of the building envelope
reference local anthropomorphic tribal masks and other
archaeological remains found in the Amazon region and
are generated by its interaction with the movement of
the island. The outermost part of the building is connected to the farthest ends of the island via stretched
structural fibers made from tree roots. The structural
fibers create thin suspended bridges and provide access
to the island. Any shifts or alterations to the growing
landscape have an immediate effect on the stability of the
building, its form, and the interaction between inhabitants
and the surrounding scenery.

Counter to the traditional form of local habitations—
called *maloca*—which are typically arranged in a circle
around a central ceremonial patio, here the dwelling capsules are organized vertically. Inspired by native
rubber-curing techniques, the envelope of the pods is
dynamic and constantly under production: a fire derived
from burning green, acid-rich palm nuts smokes the
latex, which drips constantly from the top of the highest
pod, manufacturing the envelope. Spiral frames circling
down from the top of the building form the ribcage of
the pods. The dripping latex circles the spiral frames and
thickens the skin.

Procession model

Diagrammatic elevation, vertical maloca

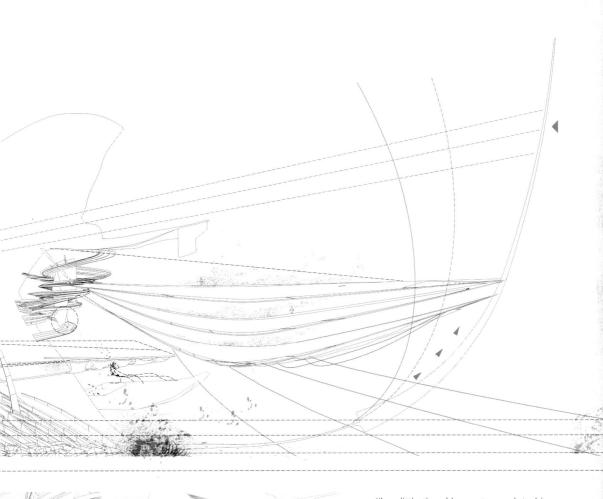

"In a little time I began to speak to him, and teach him to speak to me; and first, I made him know his name should be Friday, which was the day I sav'd his life; I call'd him so for the memory of the time; I likewise taught him to say Master, and then let him know that was to be my name; I likewise taught him to say yes and no, and to know the meaning of them."

—Daniel Defoe, *Robinson Crusoe*

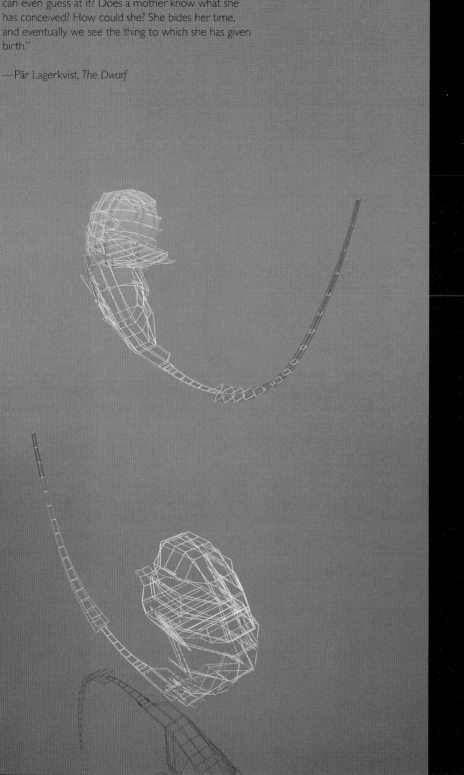

"Who knows what nature carries in her womb? Who can even guess at it? Does a mother know what she has conceived? How could she? She bides her time, and eventually we see the thing to which she has given birth."

—Pär Lagerkvist, *The Dwarf*

Impressions of the vast dam reservoir

Diagrammatic section showing water level variations

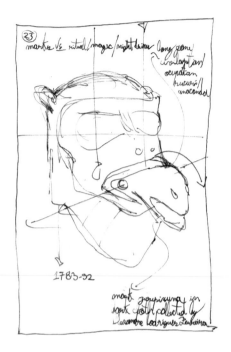

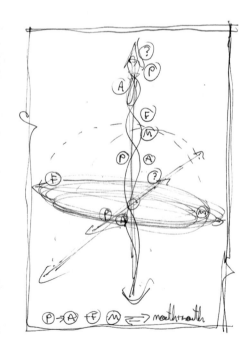

Conceptual sketches and models of native masks showing vertical organization of the maloca and its interaction with its surrounding

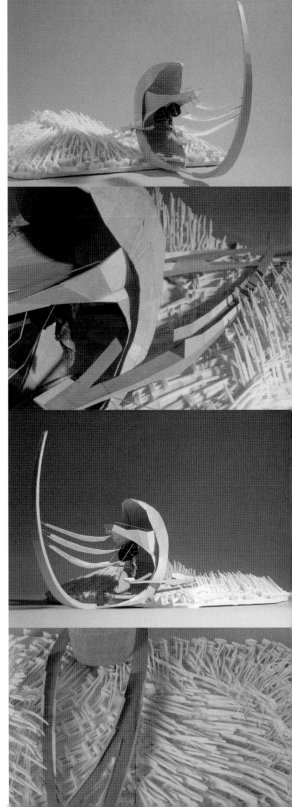

Maloca elevation at high tide

Swollen tree in the Brazilian Amazon near Tucuruí

Like the design process, the function of the project was based around a hybrid logic of fact and fiction. Counter to the conventions of architecture (i.e., problem solving dictates the design), here the design exposes and works with the contradictions and challenges faced by the uprooted native communities—to live in an island environment with significant landscape changes from winter to summer due to tide changes. Our process is one based on ongoing questioning rather than the promotion of an immutable truth for the architectural profession. We want to bolster the critical character of architecture by exploring expressive devices in language—to create an architectural counterpart to magical realism or literary irony and humor—in order to engage architecture as a reactive discipline. Architecture, like any other language, is a medium of expression, communication, and dialogue. When discussing humor in his book *Testaments Betrayed*, the novelist Milan Kundera writes:

> Humor: the divine flash that reveals the world in its moral ambiguity and man in its profound incompetence to judge others; humor: the intoxicating relativity of human things; the strange pleasure that comes of the certainty that there is no certainty.[2]

The Pregnant Island absorbs the factual and mixes it with mythical native tales. Far from creating an epic story or endorsing a return to a romanticized tribal past, the project merges existing ingredients within a spatial narrative—a space that changes with time and is a multidimensional experiment depicting cultural and social ambiguities within the context of native communities. The resulting island is not an architectonic allegory conveying a moral message but an ambiguous space that discloses the fragility of human habitat and individual choice.

[2] Milan Kundera, *Testaments Betrayed: An Essay in Nine Parts*, trans. Linda Asher (London: Faber & Faber, 1996), 32.

"Besides the above-mentioned things the people of
this place showed us another very simple thing. For
they thought that the small boats of the ships were
the children of the ships, and that the said ships gave
birth to them when the boats were lowered to send
the men hither and yon. And when the boats were
lying alongside a ship, they thought that the ships were
suckling them."

—Antonio Pigafetta, *Magellan's Voyage*

View of the pregnant island at low water level

Internal view showing circulation and
dwelling pods shaped by dripping
and thickened latex

Bibliography

We list here only the writings that have been of use in the making of this book. This bibliography is by no means a complete record of all the works and sources consulted. It indicates the substance and range of reading upon which we have formed our ideas, and we offer it as a convenience for those who wish to pursue the particular writers and fictions that are the subjects of this inquiry.

Bowers, Maggie Ann. *Magic(al) Realism*. New York and London: Routledge, 2004.

Carpentier, Alejo. *The Kingdom of This World*. Translated by Harriet de Onis. New York: Farrar, Straus & Giroux, 2006.

Coetzee, J. M. *Foe*. London: Penguin, 1987.

Defoe, Daniel. *Robinson Crusoe*. London: Penguin, 2001.

Dick, Philip K. *The Man in the High Castle*. London: Penguin, 2001.

García Márquez, Gabriel. *One Hundred Years of Solitude*. Translated by Gregory Rabassa. London: Penguin, 1973.

Gheerbrant, Alain. *The Amazon: Past, Present, and Future*. Translated by I. Mark Paris. London: Thames & Hudson, 1992.

Kafka, Franz. *The Metamorphosis*. Translated by Willa and Edwin Muir. New York: Everyman's Library, 1993.

———. *The Trial*. Harmondsworth: Penguin, 1953.

Kundera, Milan. *Testaments Betrayed: An Essay in Nine Parts*. Translated by Linda Asher. London: Faber and Faber, 1996.

Lagerkvist, Pär. *The Dwarf*. Translated by Alexandra Dick. New York: L. B. Fisher, 1945.

McEvan, Colin, Cristiana Barreto, and Eduardo Neves, eds. *Unknown Amazon*. London: British Museum Press, 2001.

Pigafetta, Antonio. *Magellan's Voyage: A Narrative Account of the First Navigation*. Edited and translated by R. A. Skelton. New Haven, CT: Yale University Press, 1969.

Rabelais, Francois. *Gargantua and Pantagruel*. Translated by M. A. Screech. London: Penguin, 2006.

Ribeiro, Darcy. *Maíra*. Translated by E. H. Goodland and Thomas Colchie. New York: Vintage, 1984.

Shiva, Vandana, and Maria Mies. *Ecofeminism*. Halifax: Fernwood Publications; London: Zed Books, 1993.

Swift, Jonathan. *Gulliver's Travels*. Hertfordshire: Wordsworth Editions, 1992.

World Commission on Dams. *Dams and Development: A New Framework for Decision-Making. The Report of the World Commission on Dams*. London and Sterling, VA: Earthscan Publications, 2000.

Acknowledgments

We would like to thank everyone who has continuously inspired, encouraged, motivated, and supported us in the preparation of this book.

In particular, we feel very much indebted to Lebbeus Woods, whose work has influenced our thinking and understanding of architecture. Many thanks to him for sharing great thoughts and ideas and contributing the foreword to this book. We would also like to express our very special thanks to Brett Steele for his continuous encouragement and support and his fantastic contribution to this book. Furthermore, we are especially grateful to Thomas Weaver for the care with which he reviewed the original draft of this book and for the helpful conversations that helped us to improve the manuscript. Special thanks also to Dr. Penelope Haralambidou and Sir Peter Cook.

For the generous support and provision of information as well as the organization of our visit to the Tucuruí Dam in Brazil, our gratitude goes to Eletronorte and Rubens Ghilardi.

And finally, many thanks also to Pamphlet Architecture, Princeton Architectural Press, and our editor, Linda Lee, for their great initiative and the faith they have consistently shown in this publication. Without their support this book would never have been possible.

About the authors

NAJA & DEOSTOS

Nannette Jackowski and Ricardo de Ostos are the principals of NaJa & deOstos, a London-based studio developed as a platform for experimental architecture. Together they are the authors of *The Hanging Cemetery of Baghdad* (SpringerWienNewYork, 2007). Their projects have been exhibited at the 6th International Architecture Biennale in São Paulo, Brazil, in 2005; the Summer Exhibition 2006 at the Royal Academy of Arts in London; and the London Festival of Architecture 2008. They are design tutors of an undergraduate unit at the Architectural Association School of Architecture in London.

Jackowski is a former project architect at Wilkinson Eyre Architects and has also worked for Zaha Hadid in London. She studied architecture at the Leipzig University of Applied Sciences in Germany and received a master of architecture degree at the Bartlett School of Architecture in London, England, under the direction of Peter Cook.

De Ostos is an architect who has worked for Peter Cook, Future Systems, and Foster and Partners. He studied architecture and urban planning at the Federal University of Minas Gerais in Belo Horizonte, Brazil, and also holds a master of architecture degree from the Bartlett School of Architecture in London, England. De Ostos has taught at Lund University in Sweden and was the curator of the Brazilian Pavilion for the London Festival of Architecture 2008.

www.naja-deostos.com

About the contributors

BRETT STEELE

Brett Steele is the director of the Architectural Association School of Architecture and AA Publications and is a partner of DAL, desArchLab, an architectural office in London. Steele has taught at the Harvard Graduate School of Design and the Berlage Institute and has lectured and led workshops throughout the world.

LEBBEUS WOODS

Lebbeus Woods is an architect who has exhibited, lectured, and published his projects worldwide and has written numerous articles of criticism about architectural practice and theory. He is the cofounder and scientific director of RIEA.ch, an institute devoted to the advancement of experimental architectural thought and practice. Woods is currently a professor of architecture at The Cooper Union for the Advancement of Science and Art in New York City.

Image Credits

Every effort has been made to track ownership and contact the copyright holders of some images used. We apologize for any omissions made and are happy to correct any mistakes and include all credits in future editions.

pp. 33, 36: From J. F. Munce. *The Architect in the Nuclear Age: Design of Buildings to House Radioactivity*. London: Iliffe Books, 1964.

pp. 38–39, 47: Eneida Castro

p. 43: Three Gorges Dam, NASA/GSFC/METI/ERSDAC/JAROS, and U.S./Japan ASTER Science Team.

Pamphlet Architecture was initiated in 1977 as an independent
vehicle to criticize, question, and exchange views. Each issue is assembled by an individual author/architect. For more information, Pamphlet proposals, or contributions, please write to: Pamphlet Architecture, c/o Princeton Architectural Press, 37 E. 7th Street, New York, NY 10003, or go to http://www.pamphletarchitecture.org.

Pamphlets published:

* out of print, available only in the collection *Pamphlet Architecture 1–10*.